19th Century Blues
Patrick McGuinness

Smith/Doorstop Books

Published 2007 by
Smith/Doorstop Books
The Poetry Business
The Studio
Byram Arcade
Westgate
Huddersfield HD1 1ND

Copyright © Patrick McGuinness 2007
All Rights Reserved

ISBN 978-1-902382-88-3
Typeset at The Poetry Business
Printed by Swiftprint, Huddersfield

Reprinted 2008

The Poetry Business gratefully acknowledges the help of Arts Council England and Kirklees Metropolitan Council.

Acknowledgements
Some of these poems appeared first in *Agenda*, *Old World Books Five Poets Series (Venice)*, *Planet: the Welsh Internationalist*, *P N Review*, *The Times Literary Supplement* and *The Yellow Nib*. 'Déja-vu' appeared as a Treganna Press poetry card, with a cover image by Alun Hemming.

This collection was a winner in The Poetry Business Book & Pamphlet Competition 2006

CONTENTS

5	*Déjà-vu*
6	The Age of the Empty Chair
7	Noon at the DoubleTree Hotel
8	The Shape of Nothing Happening
9	*Le Grand Pardon*
10	[Untitled]
11	19th Century Blues
12	Montréal
13	Daytime Drinking
14	*Spleen*: Cardiff Matchday Blues
15	Black Box
16	The Other Side
17	Montreal
18	Lists
21	The Thaw
	I – Illegible waves of wood 21
	II – Lapland 22
	III – ! ! ! 22
	IV – Stills 23
	V – writing the words 23
	VI – L O! v e 24
25	Vowels
26	The Clamour
27	*Déjà-vu*

for Charles Mundye

DÉJÀ-VU

Two tenses grappling with one instant, one perception:
forgotten as it happens, recalled before it has begun.

THE AGE OF THE EMPTY CHAIR

In Monet's *The Beach at Trouville*, it is week one of the
                               Franco-Prussian war.
The chair lodges in the sand between two women.
                               One reads, the other

points her face at the emptying beach. The chair belongs to
                               no-one,
it is a found chair, a *trouvaille*, and there is never
                               one chair too many

but one sitter too few. A flag rigid on its pole indicates
a swelling in the air, or something stronger, and the rent waves,

delicate turmoils of spume and lace, are distant cousins
                               of the revolution
bound into the ebb and flow it breaks free of, then breaks
                               back into.

There is sand in the paint; the place is mixed into its making
and even the brushstrokes replicate the water's peaks as they take

the light: roofs pell-mell across a city skyline, flashpoints in the sun.
The chair suggests all that can be suggested about change, but it
                               remains

apart from it: the way a sail suggests the wind, the way
                               a shell holds
a recording of the waves even as the waves turn around it.

NOON AT THE DOUBLETREE HOTEL

From here the river looks like a road
surprised by its own keen swerve, the boaters
stitching the water's skin as above them a Boeing
rends the sky and the sky heals over.

It's all inaudible through the triple-
glazed panes, but by something in that improbable
clear blue we know it's heavy with noise,
drenched in spent jet fuel,

and the bright blue emptiness
is emptiness only, a desert of burned-off ozone
where the sun's ferocious waste scatters
its perfect, equalising light.

Shadows straighten up, level
with the shapes that threw them – house, high-rise,
Hummer – then disappear; and for a moment
all is its original, unencumbered self.

The clock's hands cross.
The two halves of the day come face to face.
The grainy, detailed hours have reached their zenith,
now they fall away.

THE SHAPE OF NOTHING HAPPENING

Dust knows the places we have forgotten, or we never see,
marking out the margins of our world: the windowledge's
cracked paint, the bevelled edges of a doorframe,
the dado rails, the skirting boards, stifling the emphatic

corners of our lives. It fills the gulf behind the sofa,
that small domestic void that stands for losing and forgetting,
or for finding once again. It stands for things
that outlive their necessity; for us busily outliving

ours – particles slow dancing in a slant of light
shedding the excess that each day we renew.
Its tininess is a feat of scale, but it cannot disappear.
It is the shape of nothing, the shape of nothing happening,

and of nothing's impossibility; matter worrying away
at trying not to be, and being all the while; reminding us
there are no absolutes, that all is graded on the scale,
that all is incremental, deciduous, and undecided.

LE GRAND PARDON

(after notes by Rilke)

We talk, but what do we know?
Somewhere the Angel of Oblivion,
radiant, leans his face into the wind
that turns our pages.

[UNTITLED]

(after notes by Rilke)

As Venetian glass
from the moment it is born
knows this shade of grey
the uncertain light that catches it

so your gentle hands
knew in advance
they were the scales that weighed
the fullest of our hours.

19th CENTURY BLUES

Those were the days, though not for those who lived them.

Flaubert's people were at the heart of things,
the eye of the nineteenth century's storm.

Still it passed them by:

>   *

Fresh from slipping the Maréchale one Frédéric returns
to the woman who, though she does not know it,
lives only inside his head.

Even to herself she is no more than half-there,
however totally described.

The language enfolds her. Later it embalms her.

>   *

The men are rudderless, bobbing like those balloons
that overflew the siege of Paris:
they roll on frictionless, leaving holes in the air.

Minnows caught in the slipstreams of their own stories,
they tremble for a moment upcurrrent, then are gone
into the next instalment, the next word.

MONTRÉAL

The letters on the Departures Board
are falling back into themselves: London
into Montreal via three brisk ripples
of the alphabet, Amsterdam, and six hours
in the air.

      Six hours later, on the Arrivals Board,
the letters are falling back into themselves:
Montreal collapses into London and returns
as *Montréal*; as if the French passed through
a fording of the English to find itself more French.

DAYTIME DRINKING

First sip: gentle as a stream overreaching,
supple as a rope-bridge in the air;

The second, long as the creak of floorboards,
firm as a leg-iron clasp;

The third: sudden as the trap door beneath you,
the stumbling slide back to thirst.

SPLEEN: CARDIFF MATCHDAY BLUES

(some way after Baudelaire)

These arcades are no *Arcadia*; steel glades
whose girdered glass matches the angle of the rain;
matches, too, its colour – the colour of pigeons,
tanks, the dishwater sluicing the drains

as the streets gargle their litter.
There's a shop closed on every corner.
There's a shop cloned on every corner.
In all the papers, deficit, terror, loss,

and at home, deficit, terror, loss.
Plastic bags ride the wind, hoisted in surrender.
Here it is always half-time, where the stopped
clock gets it right
                            pretty much all day.

BLACK BOX

Every crashed marriage has its black box, the blow-
by-blow account of what went wrong and how,
the crescendo of mistakes that peaks, is for an instant
quiet on its crest of trauma, then drowns itself and us

in a cascade of static. The black box is what survives;
anthracite gleaming in the wreckage where, preserved in anger,
the voices that it holds replay their lifetime of last moments
and speak of how, until the very end, it might all have been

so different; and how, right from the start,
                              they knew it never would.

THE OTHER SIDE

> *… that eventless realm, neither cold nor hot, neither hilly nor flat, where the dead, each at their own best age and marooned in an eternal afternoon, pass the ages with sod all going on.*
>
> *Hilary Mantel,* Beyond Black

The dead flit lightly by. They have no ballast,
nothing can keep them down. Slowly,
like Zeppelins on the horizon, or thoughts
coming into view, they go about our lives.

Death has not altered their priorities.
They keep things in perspective.
They are as down to earth as ever,
shop locally, mow their universal lawns.

Around them a civil breeze of trespass
rustles in the trees, bends the flowers
in their flowerbeds, pries their shutters
open as the darkness rolls in from our day.

But they are not nostalgic. 'Life goes on'
they seem to say – 'all is much the same:
Eternity is just a small town age
and Night a darker shade of beige.'

MONTREAL

Un hiver dans un hiver… a winter within a winter.
The idea holds but the English lets the wordplay go:

a universe within a universe, a symmetry of
interleaving lives that, like the leaves themselves,

tells of precision married off to transience,
form that finds fulfilment in anonymity.

The snow starts soft and intimate as marrow,
climbs down winter's ladder, and finishes

as mud or mulch as tyres and gritters
mash it back to its beginnings.

It is as if something in ourselves had burst
into the air; an explosion of all our privacies.

LISTS

(for Sarah)

    I

Those last few weeks were in a way the first;
at any rate, the first we'd really got along:
three decades' tension, stretched and racked across
our adolescence, his short life's lifelong
disappointment…

But there was hardly time;
for us to make our peace with him, for him
to make peace with himself; though there was
always plenty for regret, recrimination, for things
that took time from us and gave nothing back.

    II

One day he made a list of all the things
he was sorry he'd never do again.
Most of them he'd never done at all; the rest
he'd never liked in any case. But dying
does that, knowing that the light at the end
of the white foreshortened corridor
is not the world outside, but something
outside the world.

    Then the walks along the ward,
looking for those worse off, someone to feel
better than; short walks on shortening breaths,
as he drowned in his own lungs, to the last self-
consumed.

The cancer spread like fury,
the way his anger would take hold,
would fill his lungs, the house, our lives.

III

Unlovable as ever, yet he was brave,
with that aura of unshared suffering
that spared us everything but grief at knowing
what we felt was not exactly grief.

IV

His skin like paper, that first X-ray was his watermark;
the shadow he had cast, he now cast inside himself:

death's stamp, grey against the window,
daylight burned away by one dark star.

V

Even now, even at the end, it was better left unspoken.
All my anger decompressed in those last weeks,

because I knew they were the last. I was lost
without it; he lost at no longer finding it in me.

VI

You'd recall:
his refusal to cave in to optimism,
the palliatives of mind and body
that would just extend the run-up to the night.

And I:
how easily he let it go, his life of graft
and grudging drudgery, the days racked

up on his mind's prison wall, *tomorrow
and tomorrow and tomorrow…*

but that last day there was only one.
Then nothing. None.

THE THAW

a sequence of dispoetry after Christian Dotremont

I – Illegible waves of wood

The wood's illegible waves on the desk
as you write. The first principle of form:
the wave, rings of a dropped stone.

A ridge of water, muscle stretching
in ever greater circles,
gathering in what lies around,

gathering up the stream it is part of.
So the rings of a tree: the tree ages,
thickens into the space around;

marks its past concentrically.
It remembers itself: flesh over flesh,
core hardening to rind,

becoming its own record;
drawing in the years to lay them
side by side in space, in time.

II – Lapland

The trees are exclamation marks,
the snow a long white knotted cry.

A forest of geometry,
every flake locked into its neighbour;

a polar hive, walls flush as well-
laid bricks. Each minute of the day

in place: the eye, round as the world,

sees in waves: fractals, pixels, jpeg,
the plasma screen, white busy against white.

III – ! ! !

Sleighs harvest the silence.
The cabins breathe in/ breathe out.

The boats are flying in upended sky,
ice-breakers clean their beaks on clouds of rye.

The hiss and suck of the thaw
angles becoming curves, diamonds becoming tears.

IV – Stills

The bubbles rise like stitches in the glass:
threading the spirit to the body,
winding the water round the wine.

Fire and ice, ice and fire:
take away the bottle and the drink still stands,
shoulders braced against the air.

V – writing the words

… as they move along the page
the virtual/
the vellum, cursor skimming
the blue ripples of the laptop;

the quill slides,
the electric ink of its wake.

Disks glint, stacked in their archives
of ice. The paper dreams of the wood,
the grain implicit beneath
 – between – its skin.

VI – L O! v e

Return journey to the void
via plenitude.
My bad luck. Nobody gets off here
but me.
The fourteenth station.

I love you historically
who gave me everything you had
save nothing.

Note
Christian Dotremont (1922-1979) was a Belgian poet and artist. He founded the Belgian Revolutionary Surrealist Circle, and in 1948 co-founded the CoBRA group of artists, which took its name from Copenhagen, BRussels, Amsterdam. He retained a lifelong fascination with 'nordicity', and lived for extended productive periods in Lapland. 'Dispoetry' is a translation of his term 'Dépoésie'. His complete poems are published by Mercure de France, with an introduction by Yves Bonnefoy.

VOWELS

(after Rimbaud's 'Voyelles')

A black
        E white
                I red
                        U green
                                O blue
                                        v o w e l s.
One day I'll explain your coming into being:
A, black velvet, corset of fizzing bluebottles
Weaving through a maze of stink,

Gulfs of darkness; **E**, tents, white vapours rising,
Proud glaciers lancing the sky, shivering lace;
I, purples, spat blood, the beauty of lips furious
And laughing, lips drunk with repentance;

U, cycles, divine vibrations of viridian seas,
Peace of beast-strewn pastures, alchemy's
Stamp of peace on wrinkled studious brows;

O, the last Trumpet's strange and strident call,
Silences crossed by Angels and by Worlds:
O the Omega, the violet ray of His Eyes.

THE CLAMOUR

The clamour is always just a thought away,
one wrong turning of the mind. I hear the cries
(they're mine) at the foot of a stair,
the end of a supermarket aisle,

and then it washes over in a tide of loss. All
gives way to chaos, or to what is always there:
that locked-out self that treads its mill of grief
waiting for her dying to die down.

DÉJÀ-VU

Forgotten as it happens, recalled before it has begun:
two tenses grappling with one instant, one perception.